POETRY MY WAY

By

Virginia Ames Jorgenson

Happy Reading,
Virginia Ames Jorgenson

POETRY MY WAY

By
Virginia Ames Jorgenson

Copyright © 2016
By Virginia Ames Jorgenson
Published by Gray Bonnets Press

All rights reserved. No part of this book may be reproduced or transmitted in any form or by any means electronic or mechanical, including photocopying, recording, or by any information storage and retrieval system without written permission from the author, except for the inclusion of brief quotations in reviews.

Cover design, interior and graphics
Virginia Ames Jorgenson
Gray Bonnets Press

Printed in the United States of America

Acknowledgements

What a pleasure it is to have loved ones proof your work. My sister Betty Schram is one of those people who supports while pointing out what we call "typos" rather than blatant mistakes. Thank you Betty, I love you.

Then there is my dear friend Warren Woods, whom I didn't ask to proof this time, but he was there encouraging me every step of the way. Thank you Warren, You're a sweetheart.

I like poetry that is easy to understand and relate to. I am not one to write several pages of one poem; my poems are mostly short and to the point. I hope you enjoy reading them as much as I did writing them.

Birthdays

A Birthday Gift For My Sister Betty

Eat lots of birthday cake
Tomorrow you may diet
Who knows you may need the sweets
To keep your stomach quiet

For your tummy could betray you
While you're walking in the woods
Picking up stones and twigs
And other fancy goods

If you don't find those things
Your arts and crafts may fail
Then, Betty Dearest, what would you do
Turn old and grow quite frail

Then the world would never know
Of your great gift and talents
The clever things you make and paint
Which are to me resplendent

And so my darling sister
Ice cream and cake eat hardy
You see the dire need to
Party, party, party

Betty is a crafter and often finds her supplies in the woods by her house. She sells them in various shops in her area.

Birthday Cards

I have so many cards
I don't know what to do
I have so many cards
They came from all of you
I have so many cards
Most are happy, none are blue
I have so many cards
Thank you, thank you, thank you

I wrote this after my seventy-fifth birthday and the "many cards" I received. It sure made me feel good. A simple thing like getting a card from someone can go a long way to brighten your day.

Birthday Party

Never had a party
It seemed the thing to do

Little Suzie had a party
Got lots of presents too

Another year went by
It made me kind of blue

I turned seventy this year
And with a great deal of ado

They gave an elegant party
It was worth the wait
Thank you

When I grew up it wasn't that many years since the Great Depression. As people were beginning to recover along came World War II. My family didn't have the extra money for birthday parties. We did, however, have family dinners where we could choose what we wanted for the menu. I used to ask for hot dogs, but Mama suggested I choose something different. I picked stewed chicken and dumplings, green peas and Angel Food cake with chocolate frosting for dessert.
I still like those choices.

To Gloria

You're turning seventy,
So what, big deal
Seventy is just a number
It's how you feel

If you see a bag here
And a little sag there
And silver streaks
Showing in your hair

And you think your
Bottom is not as fit
And your abs are giving
An absolute fit

So what, we say
Who really cares?
It is what you are
Inside of there

From our point of view
All we see
Is a pretty face
And sweet personality

This was written for my friend's birthday. She was a little concerned about reaching the ripe old age of 70. Now she's headed toward 80 and isn't in the least concerned.

Love and Romance

A Novel Romance

She opened the invitation
Smiling with delight
As did I

She wore silk and satin
With delicate white lace
Just like me

She danced and danced
By the light of the moon
As I swirled about my bedroom

He tenderly kissed her cherry lips
In the same way he tasted mine
His kiss increased, a most sensual thing

I blush to think of it now
Embarrassed she pushed him away
Not knowing what to do

Later as the sun went down
She glided before her bedroom mirror
My basse danse was one of romance

I made that very clear
She extinguished her oil lamp
Snuggled beneath her comforter

I lay down my book to slumber
A smile upon my face

In the 15th and 16th centuries the basse danse, or "low dance", was popular in the courts. The word basse means slow and gliding. It was a dance where the feet stay on the floor. It sounds romantic don't you think?

Love

You'll Never Know
How Much I love you

Your voice echoes
Like music from above
Your smile warms me
Through and through

How can I prove
The depth of my love
There'll be no other
In my arms, but ...

I saw you in the park
The way she looked at you
It nearly broke my heart
Your fingers brushed her cheek
Such a tender touch

Forgive me Lord
For my sinful thoughts
Desire burns inside my heart
His sensuality has
Turned away from me
And my soul cries out in pain

How it hurts when you think someone loves you and then you learn they don't.

Dating Game

Like high school all over again
She tells them, they laugh and chide

He's 83, much too old for me
I'm only 73, don't you know

Another's handsome and athletic
Would he want with a gal like me?

Can't be choosy, not many left
But like she said, she's only 73

This was taken from an overheard conversation in McDonald's. Two women were discussing the difficulty of dating. It sounded like one of them was willing to go out with anyone as long as she had a man.

Love and Adoration

Prism rays linger
In my heart
Streams of love
They impart

Sending forth
My adoration
To you, my child
The next generation

Accept it please
With hands of bliss
These streams of love
You do not want to miss

Poetry has a wonderful way of allowing us to express our feelings.

Summer Heat

Summer heat endeavored to
Prevent their romance
But it failed that evening
So very long ago

She looked at him through
Starry eyes, eyes that
Rivaled the nighttime sky
Pouring forth a promise

Startled he backed away
Her hand still on his
Shoulder, enticing
Was he ready?

Ah, but the promise
How could he resist
She smiled, amused
Knowing her man

With innate allure
Eyelashes swept down
To gently rest
Upon her tender cheeks

He was lost when they
Lifted and she looked at
Him with soft appeal
Moving forward he

Took her in his arms
She sighed and he lied
About their future together
And neither cared

This was written in my era of reading romance books.

True Marriage

After two weeks of
Wedded bliss she
Dons her negligee
And slips between
The sheets of
Their marriage bed
Only to expel an
Odorous missive

Startled
He moves aside
To give her
A look of incredulous
Surprise

Then laughter fills the room
At last the marriage
Well past consummation
Relaxes and humor comes to life

Someone told me about this type of thing and I thought it was so funny, so I wrote about it.

Seduction

Lips hover
Longing to entwine
Breath lingers
Caught inside

I dream of you
My dear in this
Whatever happens
Will be pure bliss

In this I'm certain
No doubt ensues
So come to me
My love, my muse

My goodness, this is certainly enticing and romantic, I can't believe I wrote it.

To My Grandchild

I checked my mail the other day
And much to my chagrin
The five or so that I received
Had naught but bills within

At other times it seems to me
My mail is often fraught
With requests I buy some cards
That I have never sought

Then again at Christmas time
The charities bemoan
That they are nearly broke again
And they don't want a loan

They want my money, as do I
But my heart goes out to them
I dig out my purse and scratch out a check
And in the mail I send

I would love to get a letter
From anyone will do
Instead of all the bills and junk
When will I get one from you?

I was just giving my granddaughter a little nudge a few years ago when she was away at college.

Unrequited Love

It was a cold and stormy night
As I braved the wind with all my might
To reach the dark and threatening shore
To find the one my heart adored

He stood almost within my reach
Then he walked away on the rocky beach
To embrace another with lofty speech
Tearing my heart as it fell at his feet

Life and love can be tough if you let it be.

Happy Anniversary

"I love you," says Liz
Larry replies, "Me too,
Our love is forever,
Just me and you."

Forty-six years,
It is hard to believe
That it all began with a
Look, touch, kiss and squeeze

While not always easy
To this we must attest
But it's worth it all
Considering the rest

Your love for each other
And a family to be proud
You've been richly blessed
With what the Lord has allowed

Larry and Liz have since passed away, but they'll always be remembered.

Arlene and Jim

As children you met
Soon a date you set

The years moved along
Your marriage was strong

Your kids came and went
Much joy they have lent

Then to your surprise
It is retirement time

You move to the lake,
Not a mistake

Now fifty years have passed
Happy anniversary

These friends still live at the lake and they are now well past their fiftieth anniversary and still enjoying life together.

Mama and Papa

A Night to Remember

Sitting beside the Christmas tree
She struggles with a child's delight
The scent of evergreen wafts throughout
And mistletoe winks from on high

Looking up she smiles to see
Who holds the gift of assurance
My love, my life, she calls him
As she struggles to arise

Christmas Eve, a time of hope
The eve before He came
This night of all nights
When deity unveils itself

Looking into His depth
To never let Him go
Her comforter and might
Her past and her future

This was written with my hardworking mother in mind. I can still see Mama and Papa putting our Christmas gifts together to place under the tree. I peeked.

This I Regret

Wednesday Night Fights
His favorite thing to
Watch on his new
Muntz 12" TV screen

Bent over his workbench in the
Dank basement of our house
Bluing gun barrels and
Checkering stocks

Hunting and fishing
Now that was the life
Sunburned and tired
A smile upon his ruddy face

Black hair, blue eyes
Deep cleft in chin
Man of the house
King of his castle
And I loved him

"Your mother is better looking
Than all of you put together"
He'd tell his four daughters
Usually his pride and joy

His heart attack came
When I was eleven
Another when I was eighteen
A year later his heart gave out

"He lived a long and full life"
I said at the funeral
His friends looked at me strangely
Fifty-two seemed old to me then

It was a month before I cried
And cried and cried
I feared I would never stop
But I did—in time

At first I saw him everywhere
Running to check, but no
He was gone with his
Tenor voice and whistling songs

Silly jokes and cartoon drawings
His good white shirt, the one
I wore after he left for work
His hunting, fishing and workshop

My sorrow and tears were
For me and my loss, not for
Mama, who lost her husband
And best friend
This I regret

This was about Papa. He died from his third heart attack when he was only fifty-two. I regret that I didn't spend more time with him and asking questions about his early years.

At the Pearly Gates

I do not know how she did it
Working most of her adult life
To put bread on the table
Purchase Buster Brown shoes
And later Warner's bras
"They are the best," she would say

My sister Betty and I walked home
From school for lunch one day
Mama was working in her garden
"I took the day off because I
Missed you girls"

My heart leapt in my thin chest
We ate tomato soup and
Grilled cheese sandwiches, we
Talked and laughed
It was hard going back to
School that day

She loved telephone conversations
Chats over the backyard fence
Going for family rides in the country
Eating ice cream cones and
Walking—it seemed she could
Walk forever and never tire

She canned tomatoes and peaches
Made jellies and jams
And the best cupcakes
With edges to crack off and eat
Stewed chicken with
Dumplings, my favorite

She raised African violets and canaries
Don't let the bird get out she'd
Call as we raced out the
Front door oblivious to her
Hard work and dreams

Pneumonia nearly took her
She writhed from side to feverous side
Keep the children in, it's too cold outside
But it wasn't cold
She was just chilled, poor thing

Gall bladder problems took their toll
For most of her years
You're anemic, can't do surgery
So she suffered with the
Throbbing pain until the gallbladder
Died along with the wretchedness

She wrote poetry and crocheted
Knit, sewed clothing and cooked
Washed, ironed, mangled sheets
Took care of everyone and
Papa until his third heart attack
Took him at age fifty-two

Her strong faith kept her going
She never complained
Unappreciated then, but not now
Wish I would tell her, but
I will when I meet her again
Someday at the pearly gates

My mother was such a dear. She worked full time and then came home and did all of the things I mentioned in the poem, and more. It's sad but true that when we are young we don't appreciate all that our parents do for us.

Mama Said

If I told you once
I told you a thousand times
How many times did I hear that
From Mama's lips

She meant it of course
She had said it a thousand times
Now that she is gone
And I am an adult

I think I finally understand
Having had children helped
Becoming a mama myself
Has changed my thinking

So I say to my children
The ones I love more than life
If I told you once
I told you a thousand times

In my heart of hearts I say
You are beautiful
God created you in His image
And I love you a thousand times

It is impossible to express a parent's love for their offspring, those precious ones who spill milk and dirty guest towels. Still, we love them more than life.

Mouse

Andrew is the mouse
That lived in our house
He wandered the walls at night

As I lay in my bed
I could hear his tread
Up and down and left to right

When I awoke in the AM
I told of the mayhem
It gave my Mom quite a fright

She told my Pa
Who laughed till he saw
It was not a joke in her sight

So he left the room
To look for a broom
And then he turned with a pause

To the garage he went
For a trap that was bent
On catching a mouse in its jaws

Slathered with cheese
The mouse it would please
As he reached for it with his paws

The trap snapped with delight
Soon Andrew was a sight
With his tail caught in the trap's maws

Pa picked up the trap
With Andrew intact
And brought him to the park

There he let the mouse go
Andrew ran, not too slow
As he headed for a spot that was dark

Now tonight I will sleep
Never hearing a peep
From the mouse that ran walls as a lark

The house where I grew up was inundated with mice one fall. Papa was the one to rid our home of the little pests. It took quite a while because we were soon to learn that a house never, ever has just one mouse.

Life Such As it is

Tears

Blink, wipe
Still they come
I abhor them

Necessary
You say
Still unwanted

Throat tight
Nose red
Eyes bleary

They change
Nothing
Just complexion

I have plenty
More than enough

This was written when my husband developed lung cancer from smoking. I asked him one day if he was sorry that he had smoked for so many years. I was surprised when he said, "No, I enjoyed every one of them." Well that may be, but I didn't enjoy burying him seven years ago.

Ambition

To be like God is man's ambition
Power and wisdom his pompous goal
Humble yourself is God's admonition
Lest your sinful nature destroy your soul

I wrote this for part of a composition while in college. Apparently, those were my cynical years.

Caretaker Woes

Twisting, turning
Dark alleys of fear
Steep cliffs overlook

Green meadows
Sun-driven smiles
Colorful petals that
Last for a while

Falling, falling
Drifting away
To places unseen
Soon to stay

My brother-in-law has Alzheimer's disease and my sister visits him twice a day to make sure he's being well taken care of. She is remarkable and so sweet and caring to him. She says, "He's a different person now, but I love this one too."

Conversion

Secret pictures from the past
Tearing through his mind
Things he'd rather not remember
Lest they make him blind

To the cares of those around him
Those he says he loves
Yet those secret pictures
Are divisive from above

Now he bows his head in prayer
Asking to forgive
All those secret pictures
So this new life he may live

I heard about a man years ago who apparently became addicted to porn on the computer. A few of his male friends took him under their wings and helped him through this difficult time.

Crime and Deception

It seems a mighty curse on us
Or perhaps a nasty joke
That politicians have to run
For an office that is smoke

Smoke I say for it is true
They don't want us to know
The way of things and how they work
Which at best is very low

I know that low is just a word
It is the smoke that hurts us now
For in the screen of it I see
Shadows of our futures blows

Tacking this on that to pass
Bills causing us to cringe
Shame makes us want to run and hide
Oh what we've done to our children

Waste of land and air I see
A painful curse upon our souls
Crime and violence that abounds
Because of the smoke from below

Politics! What more can I say?

If Nothing Else

This is my shelf she
Proudly said looking down at
Her protruding bosom
As she removed
Crumbs left by the muffin
She had consumed just
Minutes before

Leaving a portion of egg yoke
That refused to move
After she had licked her napkin
In an attempt to wipe the
Sticky, yellow substance
Off the shelf
She finally gave up

The family matriarch
Looked upon her retinue
To discern their opinions
Of her behavior
Seeing none, she continued
It is important to make
Negatives into positives

Now take these humungous
Appendages here, she said
Looking down with a frown
They are uncomfortable
And difficult to cover
Still they have their uses she smiled

When I was young my
Husband thought them
Very attractive
Something he never
Got over and I noticed
Several other young men
Thought the same

They were useful for my
Children's nourishment
As babes
Always there to sooth and
Comfort the young
As tears fell upon
These large soft orbs

While it is true
Straps dig into tender flesh
Proper fit seems
Impossible, yet
They exist for a purpose
Right now I am happy to say
As a shelf
If nothing else

Taking something that doesn't suit you and making it into something good. Positive thinking is extremely important if you are to survive in this world.

Life

"I'm scared" he said,
In his fright,
Not of death
But of life

Relax my friend,
It's nothing to dread
Better to live
Than to be dead

To live is to feel
To laugh and to cry
Sometimes in anguish
But not to die

Life may bring
Some stress it is true
But life can be handled
By someone like you

So forget about fear
Life's not fun that way
Keep looking up
It's a wonderful day

It's all about what we tell ourselves.

Bedtime

I have a charming little lamp
With a nightlight in the base
I love to gaze upon it
When life gets hard to face

I have a soft pink nightgown
With flowers here and there
I fancy sweet dreams as I wear it
When the night is cold and bare

I have a light green blanket
That keeps me safe and warm
I cuddle beneath it in my bed
To stave the winter storm

In the morning crisp and clear
I breathe the pleasant air
I think how grand it was last night
To be in bed till morning fair

There is something about being in your pajamas and snuggling in your bed when you are worn out from the day's events and the stresses therein.

Wife of Dementia

Where can she go in order to survive
What life has chosen as their fate?

Dimmed eyes watch and taunt
The shadow of dreams past never to return

Each day tramps on marred
With confusion and frustration, futureless

She weeps as he slowly dies
Imprisoned in his captive shell

Caretakers of people with dementia have to deal with its difficulties day after day, never knowing what to expect of their loved one. It is heart wrenching.

The Other Side

Follow me through to the other side
Not what they want you to see
If you desire to learn about life
The other place is reality

Follow me through to the other side
In order to get the full scoop
Of all the shame and all that dirt
That should make a sorry head droop

Follow me through to the other side
Though truth may be hard to observe
You say you don't want to go
When it is so blatantly served

Follow me through to the other side
The voice of reason rings out
No, no, they cry, I don't want to go
I would rather stick with my doubt

Follow me through to the other side
Where hunger and death abound
Where the sting of tears and despair
Cry out for the dawn to be found

Follow me through to the other side
Let compassion and empathy rule
Quickly now, tear down the walls
And absolve the control of fools

Follow me through to the other side
It is important we all do our share
To alleviate the atrocities
I look forward to seeing you there

I think that we choose to complain while we do nothing to research what goes on behind the scene in politics realm.

NATURE And PETS

Loyal Love

I'm in the kitchen writing
The only one who's up
Except for my dog Sunbeam
A truly exceptional pup

She appears to be sleeping
But she keeps one eye on me
It's said that dog is man's best friend
Because of loyalty

That criterion she has met
And others along the away
Like when she endures our long talks
Before she gets to play

With her fluffy tail waging
And a golden smile upon her face
She greets me upon awakening
With a clever dance in place

She growls and sometimes scolds me
And sneezes when she's told
She's been a pal for many a year
But now she's getting old

At times a little stiff
With her aches and pains
She gets up from her nap
Pleasing me her only aim

She senses my attention now
One eyebrow up and then the other
She slowly yawns and stretches
And comes over to her mother

She rests her head upon my lap
And puts a paw up too
Her eyes look softly into mine
They seem to say *I love you*

I gently stroke her silky coat
And shake her greeting hand
"I love you too" I say
"Sunbeam, you're my special friend"

Sunbeam was our golden retriever. When we would go for walks the long hair on her haunches would sway back and forth. She was truly a beautiful dog inside and out.

Bobber

It slides through the water
With no grace at all
That red and white something
Shaped like a ball

I watch and watch it
And all that I see
Is its colorful bobbing
In the waves near me

But bobbing is not
What it's meant to do
Its job is to sink
With a fish or two

Whether graceful or not
I continue to stare
At the red and white bobber
While my hook dangles bare

If you're a fisher person you know what I mean.
Perch have a way of grabbing the worm and you never know it.

Butterfly

Parchment, stained-glass wings
Flutter among the flowers
In the months of summer, fall and spring
Granting life between the showers

It is difficult to choose or say
Which amongst their formal attire
Offers the most colorful array
Hues of gold and reds of fire

Wings whisking here and there
Plucking pollen fresh and moist
Blossoms bursting in the air
Bringing forth fruition of choice

God has a way with His creation that both thrills and amazes me. Butterflies are a good example of that.

Her Pup

Her voice rang out, but not with alarm
A precious puppy she held in her arms
Look, look I want you to see
My puppy's love and it's all for me.

She put the pup down to scamper away
Chasing him throughout the day
The puppy ran with all its might
Wagging his tail in great delight

When evening came both were worn out
The voice that rang was without a shout
Just a sweet sigh and then a moan
As the two went to bed with nary a groan

Puppies and children are so delightful to watch.

Floral Petals

She spreads her lush
Petals
For all the world to see

Pink, coral, red,
Blue and more
In whorls of ecstasy

Bursting forth in exquisite masses
Among the rocks
And marshy grasses

To fill the air with her sweet scent
And thrill the eye for all who see
One small gift that God has sent

Is there anything more beautiful than wild flowers gracing the land? I think not.

Skipper

Martha Mop
I called her just for fun

She found us one day
When she was young
In her shaggy black coat
Barefoot and pregnant

No one wanted her
I know, I checked

She moved right in
Making herself at home
Then she presented us
With three wee ones

First the color of chocolate
The second white as snow
The last black and shaggy
A near replica of her

They were noisy and demanding
She loved them anyway
They were, after all,
Her only off-spring

For seventeen years
She graced our home
With joy and laughter
She gave us all she had to give

Then she died
And I cried

The wonderful thing about pets like Skipper is that they love us despite our frailties and because of this they enhance our lives.

Squirrel

Running through the trees
Leaping to and fro
Sometimes scratching fleas
Large black eyes aglow

Furry tail held high
Cocking head a-jaunt
"Come on and play outside,"
The little creature taunts

But it is cold out there
And it is snowing too
I might get wet
Or even catch the flu

Life's much too short for that
And yet at times it can fall flat

While sitting at my kitchen table looking out the sliding glass doors I saw a squirrel having the best time. It made me want to go out and enjoy the snow as well, but I changed my mind and wrote the poem instead.

Black Bug

Trudging across the porcelain
Of my tub
Like Channel
Black dot on white

I sit in my repose and muse
As one joins another
Single file on the edge
They plod

To nowhere in particular
Except perhaps
To create
Next year's parade

Someone told me they were strawberry bugs, but after Googling them I found out there weren't. They are just a black beetle. We got them for a short time every spring. They did no harm, just slowly walked along.

Me and the things I like

Thoughts

It is difficult to think of change
On a bright and sunny day
But when one finds it cloudy
One feels the other way

Take my Uncle George for instance
Who previously seemed all right
Is now the blooming idiot
Who forgot to turn out the light

And then there's the electric company
Whose bills seem much too high
Who can't keep power going
When a storm cloud drifts on by

Of course when it is raining
And the lightning strikes about
I have to turn off my computer
Because a microchip might burn out

And that reminds me of another thing
Something I can't stand
The calories in a potato chip
No matter what the brand

Is there no end to all the trouble
About which potatoes bring?
Like the ugly potato bug
And other mealy things

Now bugs are sure a nuisance
They draw spiders don't you know
Because spiders like to eat them
Before they bite your big toe

I stubbed my toe on a chair the other day
Now my sock and shoe won't fit
I'm stuck in the house for
A week they say

I sure wish the rain would stop
And the sun would shine again
So I can work in my flower garden
To pull the weeds and tend

Naturally the weeds grow stronger
So now I'll need to try . . .
Wait just a minute here
Is that a rainbow in the sky?

Yes it is a rainbow I am sure
Now I feel much better
I'll just grab my hat
And that charming old gray sweater

Everything looks good now
Even Uncle George
I think I'll go out to my garden
And put my gloomy thoughts in storage

I don't have an Uncle George, but he just seemed to fit in here.

Self Esteem

I want you to meet my self-esteem
A fragile character indeed
Her tentative smile and faded gleam
Not much but important to me

Sometimes she dictates what to do and wear
At others she disappears
That's when I think she's not worthwhile
A shrinking violet in arrears

I bless or sometimes scold her
Depends upon the day
"Must work upon my self-esteem,"
I am often heard to say

She needs to be pampered and fed
Built up in every way
It's a necessary thing to do
If I am to live and play

Spoiled soul that she is
Takes advantage of my flaws
But I know she wants the best for me
My esteem without a cause

We often like to blame a bad attitude on poor self-esteem. It's a good excuse, but sometimes it's a matter of forgetting about poor little me and moving on while thinking about others and making them more important than us. Personally, I just remind myself that I am a child of God, that's a pretty big deal. You can't get much better than that.

I like

I like sunshine and warm days
I like rain drops when they fall
Drizzle and mist distress me
Thunder excites my soul

I like going for rides and
Exploring new sights and sounds
And walking by the Rum River
When the day is soft and gentle

I like ice cream cones
The real kind, not soft-serve
Especially pralines and cream
In waffle cones, they're the best

I like hot fudge sundaes
Chocolate brownies
Chocolate chip cookies
I like chocolate

I like baking bread and
Kneading the dough
The smell of yeast and the
Expectation of taste

I like people young or old
Especially when they smile
I even like those
With drifting minds

I like a good night's sleep
On freshly laundered sheets
And waking in the morning
To anticipate the day

I like the Antique Road Show
This Old House, American Pickers
Pawn Stars, Holmes on Homes
And sometimes NCIS

I like to read, write
Sing, doodle pictures of
Faces, mostly women with
Curly hair, don't ask me why

I like my apartment
And the building where I live
All of the activities and
Crazy Canasta on Tuesday nights

I like my church and the
Sermons that touch me
Music if it isn't too loud
And reading the Bible

I like, no, I love Jesus
He has saved me despite
My sins and loves me still
In my unworthiness

I like the gift of life
With all its pain and suffering
The growth that comes
From lessons learned

I like good attitudes
Giving people who
Have strength of character
And are thoughtful

I like my silver van
It's free of debt
Despite its poor mileage
And the cost of repairs

I like green grass when
It peeps through the brown
After a spring rain
Offering hope to us all

I like that this list
Could go on forever
With words of joy and
Acceptance

My writers group had an assignment to write about things we like. This was my rendition. In going through it once again I realize how much it says about me and about how much I have to be grateful for.

Lilymoe

I am perfect, don't you know?
Perfect as a Lilymoe
You don't know what that might be?
Just read on and you will see.

Lilymoe feels simply divine
When the sun begins to shine
When the sky is dark and glum
Lilymoe is sort of numb

Lilymoe lives deep within
And changes with my every whim
So if I chance upon a plus
Lilymoe charges in a rush

But when my day is not so great
And Lilymoe is forced to wait
Until my spirit flares once more
Lilymoe pouts, she wants to soar

With lots of ideas well in hand
Lilymoe begins to plan
What shall we do this glorious day?
Let's clothe ourselves and go out to play

We'll fly a kite or go for a swim
Perhaps we'll take a spell at the gym
Lilymoe has lots of notions
Like maybe the kite will fall in the ocean

Sometime Lilymoe is a great thing
Yet at others I'd like to give her a sling
To outer space or further than that
But without Lilymoe, life would fall flat

Now do you know what Lilymoe is?
Have you guessed that she is more than a sieve?
Lilymoe is . . .well, you see,
Lilymoe is the emotion in me

As you can see, I was feeling rather silly when I wrote Lilymoe, but there is some truth to it.

Wrinkles

There they go
From left to right
Up and down
They're such a fright

No respect for me at all
They first reach up
And then they fall
My lips, my cheeks, they do it all

They say it's character
They say 'tis life
Well they are wrong
It is simply strife

The nerve of them
To think and say but
I guess they don't know
They'll soon look the same way

I have far too many of those crinkly things. I didn't realize when I was young that even your arms and legs could get wrinkles, too. I know it now though. If I don't laugh about it I just might cry.

My Quest

A part of me I know,
But only part,
While recesses dwell
Deep within my heart
And vast uncharted wastelands
Map my mind

I must explore,
I must explore,
And search until I find
The rest of me
Lest my soul, I fear, be lost
For all eternity

How well do we really know ourselves? Far too often we only know the surface of who we are and we fail to take the time to delve further into our psyche.

Mankind

In the depths of human reason
Floundering in mass confusion
Reaching out in desperation
Condemning God in self-delusion

The world today, at least that's the way I see it.

My Crying Room

Quiet, restful, private
Where can I find it?

In bed at night he'll hear me
In the car they will see
In the park-strange looks
At church they will console

I feel alone, is there nowhere?
Oh how my heart aches
God waits to wipe away
My tears
He, and He alone is
My crying room

When my husband was in his last days of lung cancer I wrote this poem. I needed to find a place where I could cry, but my husband was always nearby and I didn't want to upset him. In time I realized that God knew my tears and I was able to rest in Him.

My Favorite Spot

You ask me where is my favorite spot
I'm a bit embarrassed because it's not so hot
It's just a little city lot

But in the back there are some trees
Which grace me with the with a summer breeze
And in the fall the autumn leaves

Along the edge are plants of green
Hostas and ferns are often seen
With a blaze of color in between

Some days, when it is really hot
I sit upon my garden plot
And contemplate whether to or not

Transplant a flower or a pot
To another precious open spot
Or just to sit and think a lot

Today I gaze outside and see
A rabbit as cute as it can be
I wonder it is a he or she

A butterfly and a bee
Are flitting around for all to see
As they pollinate each bush and tree

The rabbit is sampling some of my beans
Of this I am not at all keen
So I shoo him away feeling slightly mean

The rabbit is gone or so it seems
Now upon my rake I lean
And take in all that my eyes can glean

I love my garden with all of it sprouts
Of which I like to brag and shout
So come on over to see what I'm talking about

After moving to a new home I again planted a garden. This time it was mostly vegetables. I was soon to learn that rabbits love peas and beans when they first pop out of the soil.

Observation

He sat with his back toward me
Reading a section of the newspaper
To his three teenage sons
Who responded with stoic faces
And hatred in their eyes

One boy, the oldest of the three
Rose from his seat without a word
Left for a while, came back and
Left a second time
Again saying nothing

The other two did not move
Nor did they speak
No give and take in this relationship
Only malice and reading aloud
To unresponsive boys

Good-looking, clean cut
Tall, athletic, very self-disciplined
And silent until the father folded his paper
"Are we done?" asked the younger boy
"Yes," so they all stood up to leave

As they walked away one of the boys
Looked at me with a tiny smile on his lips
My grandmotherly heart cried for them
Was it divorce? Abuse?
Had they done something wrong?

That is how it is at a fast food place
You cannot help but
People-watch and form stories
Out of your observations
Whether right or wrong

A number of times, while eating at a fast food restaurant, I have seen men eating with their sons. Often they appear to have nothing to say to each other. The kids look as if they can't wait to leave and the fathers have the same expression. They look so bored, which wouldn't be that way if the parent were more involved in their child's life. This makes me realize of how precious our time with our kids is; we should use it more wisely.

Perception

Sometimes I'm gray
Sometimes I'm light
Seldom am dark
Nor often pure white

This is probably best
Since we're not totally right

Because dark looks so *bad*
And white seems *pure*
The space in between
Though a mite insecure

Is most often achieved
A comfortable lure

So patience my fiend
We're all human you see
Be careful when judging
A person like me

For I'll fail you often
The "me" you perceive

Sometimes people try to put us in little boxes, but we often don't fit.

He Sent His Son

Gentle as a breeze
Wafts about my heart
Fragrant as a rose
Your love to impart

Gentle as a shower
Cleanses souls of sin
Renting of the Veil
Spiritual growth within

Bright and shining stars
Blessings from on high
Nourishment of life
Guiding from the sky

There will never be
Another God like thee
Who loved with such deep passion
That He sent His Son for me

God has done so much for me, lowly as I am, how can I not love Him?

God's Love

Isn't it just like God
To see deep within the soul
To reveal the rotten things in us
We want no one else to know

Isn't it just like God
To send His only Son
To walk us through our sinful lives
And show us what we've done

Isn't it just like God
To draw us close to Him
To cleanse our filthy rags
And make our sins grow dim

Isn't it just like God
To teach us of His love
To put His arms around us
With the wings of a dove

One day, as I sat before my computer, I thought about the greatest of all gifts, that of God's love.

Recall

I wrote a poem in my sleep last night
That left at the break of dawn
To drift at the edge of my consciousness
And taunt me all the day long

What is the purpose of dreaming
If the mind cannot recall
The thrill of the vision and fantasy
Before the start of the fall

Into psychological nightmares
Meant to frighten and scare
Strange how the poem I had written
Led me to the great nowhere

That's the way it is with poetry or any kind of writing for that matter. Sometimes we get wonderful ideas that soon escape us. Perhaps "Frustration" would be a better title for this poem.

Road to Senility

I'm on the road to senility
And going very fast
Not sure of my destination
But fear that it might last

Age spots, cellulite
Eye glasses to be sure
We won't even mention
The hair growing in my ears

My face looks like a road map
Of my many years
Oh, you'll find some smooth places
But more likely rivers from tears

Yet it doesn't really bother me
This aging I've professed
It simply tells about my life
Until I know the rest

As we grow more mature we begin to worry about losing our cognitive skills, which to some degree we do. My friends and I lament about not being able to multitask anymore. But when I think about it, I don't mind, multitasking is not something I need to do. My kids are now grown so they can take over the commission.

Other Stuff

Samples

"What a good example
Of ways to serve a sample,"
I heard a woman say

The sample server's smile
Is what has made my day

Have you ever noticed
How some begrudge the fact
That they are giving samples
Of things like this and that?

You'd think the cost was theirs
Instead of from the store
Why they even frown when
Young children ask for more

Now, I do like my samples
But not from such as she
So I shall thoroughly snub her
Much like she did me

Instead I will get my samples
From the lady with the smile
The other one when I pass her
I will turn my head a while

Not that it really matters
To one such as she,
Even with her chocolate
Or my favorite tea

Just give me a smiling lady
One with a friendly word
And I will walk a mile for her
At least that is what I heard

If you get to the grocery store at the right time you won't have to buy lunch later. I love the samples and even purchase some from time-to-time.

Saturday Morning

Snow makes itself at home
Perching gently on tired, rusty leaves
Mother Nature dares not breathe
Lest she disturb the scene
A mournful siren cries
Then all is silent
Except where the siren went

A breeze begins to stir
Whisking swirls here and there
Moaning trees stretch their arms
Exposing naked leaves
A second siren sounds
A chilling scream
Then all is silent
Except where the siren went

And as stealthily as the snow descends
A life is changed

After writing this poem, I brought it to a critique group and read it aloud. About a month later when I again attended the group a man read a poem in which he had plagiarized mine. He was a nice man so I was very surprised. I think my poem stuck in his head and when he wrote his he didn't realize what he had done. I said nothing and let it go. I liked mine better anyway.

Sophie

You've a beautiful daughter
I've had three
Each with her own
Personality

Your little girl
All bundled in pink
Will grow up so fast
That it is hard to think

You turn around
And the years have flown
You question what happened
Now that she's grown

So value those moments
And preserve them for her
For the years go so fast
That they become a blur

I know you will do it
Take pictures and such
For you love your daughter
Oh, so much

I was blessed with three beautiful daughters and nine years later a wonderful son. How I love them all.

Desert Storm

Dry, gritty, golden sand
Is all he sees as he waits
The sand seems never ending
He used to think it was like a beach

It looked that way in
The Sheik of Arab'y
But movies aren't' real
They just glamorize

The sand is rough and stony
It hurts when he falls
Into fox holes
And he cried last night

Maybe cuz he got no mail yesterday
Or the day before
Or maybe cuz they're so many guys around

And he's still lonely
And it's cold at night

Last night he heard someone crying
He's not sure why
He just did
Maybe he's lonely too

And bruised
And the sand goes on forever
And it's cold at night
But wait

Was that his name at mail call?
A large manila envelope
Less than twelve ounces

He laughs

Kool Aid, Cup-a-Soup, gum, jerky
And a note
We love you and are praying for you
He reads

He drinks the Kool Aid
Saves the soup and jerky
That Juicy Fruit sure tastes good
A soothing warmth seeps up inside

He slips the note near his heart

And the sand goes on forever
And someone's gonna cry
Cuz they're lonely
And it's cold at night

But not him
Tonight he's warm
And loved

I wrote "Desert Storm" in 1990, when President George Bush was in office, not George W., but his father. Things have changed since then with electronics and Skype and that type of communication. I'm sure they help, but being away from home and family and loved ones can't be easy for anyone.

Flu Season

I coughed until I thought I'd drop
And then I coughed some more
The old flu bug has got ya
Said the doc when he came in the door

So I took the meds he gave me
That made me sleep and snore
Until the bug had left me
Weak and pale until I got outdoors

I hope you got your flu shot! I thought I didn't need one, but I did.

Forgetfulness

She lost her mind
She's not sure where
If she looks hard enough
It's sure to be there

The harder she tries
The more she forgets
She won't miss it much
She has few regrets

Someday she knows
There'll be a need
When she looks for a flower
And comes up with a weed

But as for today
She'll let it pass
For it's only her mind
Alas, alas

I know a woman who is sure she is going to get dementia, so when she forgets something, she blames it on her perception of her future. Personally, I don't think she has dementia or ever will. Too bad she's misled herself so.

Frog

I'm glad a frog
Is not a hog
Because a hog looks like a log
With appendages beneath his sog

I'm glad a frog
Is not a dog
Because a dog
Much like the hog
Has a nose that likes to prod

I'm glad a frog
Lives in a bog
And croaks while sitting on a log
With eyes a-bulging all agog

I like this frog
But I love my God
Because my God
Has made the frog
The log shaped hog
And the prodding dog

This is such a silly poem. I wrote it for a woman who collected frog figurines.

Made in the USA
Lexington, KY
27 April 2018